The Church must do Better!

By

Rev. David Latimore

Rev. David Latimore
The Church Must Do Better

Rev. David Latimore
The Church Must Do Better

DH Publishing Company
PO Box 333
Indianapolis, IN 46250

Copyright © 2019 Minister David Latimore
All rights reserved. No part of this book may be used or reproduced in any manner whatsoever without the written permission of the publisher, except where permitted by law.

Cover design: DH Publishing Company
ISBN: **13: 978-1-7336502-1-2**
ISBN: **0: 1-7336502-1-0**
Edited by DH Publishing Company
www.dhpublishingco.com
dhpublishingco@gmail.com

Rev. David Latimore
The Church Must Do Better

Rev. David Latimore
The Church Must Do Better

Table of Contents

Prayer:	8
Acknowledgements:	10
Introduction:	12
Drama in the Church:	19
The Push Back:...............	21
Signs of Spiritual Abuse:	24
The Purpose of the Church:	28
Greed:	30
Deception & Fraud:	34
Conviction:	39
Hypocrites:	42
The Peoples Voice in the Church:..	46

Rev. David Latimore
The Church Must Do Better

Being Judgmental: *55*

Are You Serving in a Dying Church: *58*

Serving in the Ministry *63*

Change Is Very Hard: *65*

Rev. David Latimore
The Church Must Do Better

Prayer

Dear Lord, send the Holy Spirit upon us so we may have the wisdom to make the right judgment. Let us open our eyes to see what is right and what is wrong. May we treat other people with love and respect as we would like to be treated. We ask this prayer through Christ Lord. Amen.

Rev. David Latimore
The Church Must Do Better

Acknowledgement

My former pastor Michael K. Jones of Progressive Missionary Baptist Church, who is now gone home to be with the Lord. Repeatedly told us, if we don't promote yourself, promote God and he will give you the platform to speak. I served in ministry in the Indianapolis, Indiana area, and I have served most of my life in some capacity in the church. I have been married for over 20 years to Denise Latimore, and have three beautiful children, Willie, Probia, and Khari. I have also been blessed with two amazing grandchildren, Harlow and Harper.

Rev. David Latimore
The Church Must Do Better

Rev. David Latimore
The Church Must Do Better

INTRODUCTION

When I began to write this book and share my thoughts and its vision with others, it quickly escalated into "I'm just bashing the church," I started to laugh. Folks here is the reality; the church has been bashing people for years? What is bashing? The definition of bashing is as follows, harsh, gratuitous, prejudicial attack on a person, group, or subject. Bashing is a team meeting to hit or assault, but when it is used as a suffix, or in conjunction with a now indicating the subject. Being attacked is usually used to imply that the act is motivated by bigotry. So when I hear the word bashing, the first word comes to my mind is accountability. When I think about the church and the leadership, I think about the responsibility that the leader has to everyone. Often leadership of the church has failed, and they don't want to be held accountable. But it is not just the church, but any organization that has leaders, let me give you an example. Sometimes we hear or see a police officer treating a citizen badly and unjustly, and without cause, have you ever noticed no matter what police department it is, no one ever stands up and corrects the officer publicly, it's almost as if they can do whatever they want without retribution from anyone. Have you ever noticed that when a teacher is accused of sexual misconduct, no teacher has ever stood up and said anything, and when a doctor has performed surgery, improperly, have you ever noticed no doctor has ever stood up and held that doctor accountable? Notice that in the church we are so quick to call out other organizations such as the police department, politicians, and so forth, but we

Rev. David Latimore
The Church Must Do Better

don't hold our organization accountable. My word to any organization is before we began to call out someone else's organization; we should look in the mirror. I am most certainly not an advocate of challenging leadership in the church, but I'd still believe that right is right and wrong is wrong as well, and when our leaders in the church do something wrong they should be held accountable. It's incredible to me how we see time and time again that leaders in the church abuse their authority with sexual misconduct and adultery, and in some cases, the only thing people say is to pray for them. My prayer is that someone in leadership would read this book and change their ways and begin to look at people as people and not their property. God tells us to be faithful over a little, and he will make you ruler over a lot. Often when you hear this part of the scripture found in Matthew 25:23 most people will equate that with money, but we should also look at it in the light of people, some churches are not growing because they treat people without a loving spirit. Some have taken the position that God sent them a member and God will send other members; in other words, he will always provide. I don't believe that you can continue to use God's people in a wicked unloving and abusive way and God is going to give you more people. We all have heard on a Sunday morning, that if you can't love and take care of an apartment why would God bless you with a house, if you're not faithful to the five people in your congregation why do you think God will bless you with 500. It has indeed been a blessing to me to be able to go out to different churches and spread the gospel and in doing so, I have been noticing attendance in many churches across the country, and it is at an all-time low. It puzzled me, so I started observing and listening, and the question came to me, why are people leaving the church. This has stayed on my mind for quite some time now, so I decided to do some research. I reached out to the community to get their thoughts and perspective on the matter. It was amazing at how many people were so eager to give their feedback and to share some of their experiences within the church, that I was compelled to write this book. After the research and the feedback, I've concluded that as pastors, teachers, men, and women of God, we have failed our communities. Leaders should be respected leaders in the city that people look up to and whom they can come to in the time of need and understanding. But instead, some leaders have shown us that they are more concerned with fattening their pockets, committing adultery, having sexual activities with young men and women, being judgmental, rather than feeding their members spiritually with the word of God. These types of behaviors have made many stray away from the church. I am sure you are already thinking that I am bashing the church, but let me ask you this, what is the church guilty of?

The Church is guilty of bashing the LGBTQ community. It is not enough for preachers, evangelists and pew sitters to condemn, vilify, and ostracize gay people anymore. They are no longer satisfied in merely removing them from their faith communities; they now seem compelled to strip those who identify as LGBTQ of the basic rights and dignities this country affords all of its citizens.

Rev. David Latimore
The Church Must Do Better

The Church is guilty of bashing the Muslim Community. The irresponsible, politicized religious fervor that paints all those who practice Islam as dangerous, would-be terrorists, is being generated almost solely by professed Christian leaders. They are responsible for discrimination and violence against peace-loving Muslims in America and cultivating unmerited resentment toward an entire community based only on their differing religious convictions.

The Church is guilty of bashing people of color. ***Black lives matter. Black deaths matter.*** The longer Christians dig in their heels and refuse to say these words, the longer we justify violence against young black men, the more we suggest that demanding equality is somehow subversive—the more we testify to the systematic racism saturating the Church and the individual hearts of so many white Christians. We cannot hate people because of the color of their skin and be Christlike at the same time.

Rev. David Latimore
The Church Must Do Better

The Church would stop bashing women. Whether for pursuing roles as leaders in the Church, for wearing the clothing they feel comfortable wearing, for breastfeeding their kids, for desiring to have control over their bodies, organized Christianity still does not understand how to treat women with the dignity and equality they deserve. The Church desperately needs to embrace and celebrate its feminine side.

I wish the Church would stop bashing those who don't believe in God. Facing dwindling church membership, too many Christian leaders seem burdened to double-down on the war rhetoric of the insidious, evil culture beyond the church campus, to stoke the fires of urgency in the shrinking faithful. Such caricatures paint Atheists and Agnostics as less moral or less decent or less loving—and this isn't true.

Stop bashing people for exercising freedom. Whether it's not pledging allegiance to the flag, for protesting the shootings of black men by police, displaying outrage at the gun violence in our streets, demanding marriage for everyone, American Christians need to learn that freedom isn't confined only to expressions that match their conclusions. People are not anti-American, ungodly, or wrong, just because we do not agree with them.

Rev. David Latimore
The Church Must Do Better

I wish the Church would stop bashing political leaders. The lazy stereotype that imagines Jesus to be the sole property of the Republican Party is one of the most unproductive ideas we've produced in the past few decades. It denies God's presence in all people, it is nurturing division in our country, and it is invalidating the spirituality of millions of people who don't identify as G.O.P but still fully believe in G.O.D.

The Church should stop bashing the world. It's so easy to label people; to categorize them based on the way they look, talk, or pray, whether they drink, cuss, or have tattoos. Somewhere along the line, we made Christianity about producing some tidy, holy homogeneity, instead of embracing the stunning diversity of humanity. Maybe those rough edges, colorful vernaculars, and bold expressions are God itself, and they make the Church better and more beautiful.

The Church is not a building. It's the corporate expression of followers of Jesus in the world, and right now this shared testimony appears to be doing far more damage than good out there. We can't claim love for *all* people while holding disregard or absolute contempt for so many *of* those people.

It isn't Church-bashing to call the Church and the Christians who comprise it, to give the world a far better, more loving, more decent, more Jesus like reflection than it is.

The people of God need to be the people with the most tender hearts, the biggest tables, and the widest arms. The church must do better!

Church, let's start loving and stop bashing.

Rev. David Latimore
The Church Must Do Better

In my book, you will read some experiences that people have dealt with in the church. Maybe then we can come together as a whole to work toward rebuilding a relationship with trust, honesty, and loyalty with our leaders. Then and only then will we be able to heal as a community and bring God our Savior back into our daily lives and live the life where God can be pleased.

The church must do better!

Rev. David Latimore
The Church Must Do Better

Why Is There So Much Drama In The Church?

I don't know about you, but my life always seems to have enough drama in it. I certainly don't need anything that is going to add the drama factor. So often, people seek out the church because they need a reprieve, a refuge from the emotional drama. Now, I get that we're all imperfect and that any group will have conflict, but some churches seem to do drama more than others. Our jobs, family dynamics, and friendships provide us with enough opportunity to be gossiped about, back-stabbed, and pushed to the margins, and we don't need to add to that. The Church needs to be a safe place where one can escape the typical relational drama we all face, and instead experience loving support, and acceptance. When the church becomes another area that is going to add drama to peoples lives, some will cut the cord and move on for their sanity. People don't want to feel like they need to become a carbon copy of an individual or idea to be fully included and appreciated. People want to be whom God made them. They don't want to be a carbon copy of whom God made you. Some feel forced to fit into a predetermined mold as to what a member of this community must look like, people leave.

A fruit tree grows fruit, and if you choose not to pick the fruit from it, the fruit will fall off and die, and then you will be standing around wondering why you can't make a fruit pie from what's left.

The church must do better!

Rev. David Latimore
The Church Must Do Better

THE PUSH BACK

Too often people leave a church because of disagreement, not getting their way, or because the sermons are no longer deep enough. Usually, when we dig into the reason the sermons are not deep enough, it ultimately goes back to the person being offended or not having their faulty theologies endorsed from the pulpit. The same pastor who was previously deep enough becomes shallow once there is an offense. It's incredibly difficult to hear from God in a sermon when we are offended by the person delivering the sermon.

Before we quit the church, we need to make sure we take the separation seriously. The church is a family to which we belong – big difference. When we leave, we make a statement. When we go because we don't get our way, it will set a poor example for others.

Need proof? Just ask the Pharisees. They had an audience with the Son of God, but could not get past their offenses. Perception can impact the ability to trust. If we do not believe, trust the person, we will reject his message, even if the message is true.

As Christians, we should examine our motives before we make a decision. Are we running away from a problem? Is there a real issue between us and someone else? If so, have we followed Matthew 18, and talked to the person, instead of talking about the person?

Frustration is never content until it's expressed. If we have frustrations that we have not dealt with, those same frustrations will most likely follow us to the next church.

Rev. David Latimore
The Church Must Do Better

Before we leave, have we done everything we can to make peace in the situation? As a minister, I know how difficult it is to express frustrations with church leadership. It may be difficult, but Christians are called to a higher standard. Without attacking, have we expressed our concerns with the church leadership? Are we willing to get our hands dirty and become a part of the solution? Have we prayed about leaving? These are tough questions that force us to get real.

When we leave, we impact others. At times, it may even feel like a divorce. When we view the church as a family, it will change the way that we leave. If we must go, separate in a way that honors God. Often people will not want to hear from you, so you must do what the Bible tells you. Matthew 10:14 | "If anyone will not welcome you or listen to you, shake the dust off your feet when you leave that place, as a testimony against them." Staying in a church where God no longer wants you to be, can lead to spiritual abuse. The church must do better!

Rev. David Latimore
The Church Must Do Better

Rev. David Latimore
The Church Must Do Better

Signs of Spiritual Abuse

Spiritual Abuse Warning Signs
#1 Critics are Isolated

Not only are critics cut out of the spiritual abuser's inner circle they are also isolated. After all, the leader cannot afford to have critics speaking up for what they believe is right. Therefore, they do everything they can to isolate and discredit critics, smearing their character, accusing them of lacking faith, saying their **understanding of the Bible** is wrong, and even spreading lies about them. A leader is guilty of spiritual abuse and wants his followers to have nothing to do with critics and seeks to discredit them as ungodly sinners who are holding back God's plans. The sad reality is that those labeled "critics" often start as close confidants of the pastor, but once they begin to push back, they are cut off. Instead of being able to provide guardrails for the soaring ambition of a lousy Leader, they will be sidelined and slander.

Spiritual Abuse Warning Sign #2
Loyalty Is Prized Over Diversity

For a church or religious movement to be healthy, a diversity of opinions is required. In Christ, we are all priests to God, filled with the Holy Spirit, and given unique gifts to build up the church. This doesn't work for the spiritually abusive pastor or unspiritual leaders. Diversity leads dissent, which slows momentum and keeps him from achieving his grandiose plans. He doesn't want a variety of opinions. He wants loyalty. You're either in, or out, or against.

Rev. David Latimore
The Church Must Do Better

And if you're not all in, you're accused of being disloyal, and not being a team player, a naysayer, and a downer of not believing in the mission.
A sure sign that things are going downhill is when everyone in leadership thinks, acts, and even speaks alike. Additionally, if the leadership team gets smaller and smaller, it's a sign that the pastor is hoarding power and promoting only the most loyal followers.

They Refuse To Believe Anything Is Wrong
Sadly, most bad pastors refuse to believe that anything is wrong with their leadership style or the way things are headed. They remain convinced that everything is great, up until the point that everything falls apart.
Staying in a situation where you unappreciated is not called loyalty, it is called breaking your own heart. You care, and you will always care.
That's your problem. It's ungodly to stay in a hot mess regardless of what they tell you. God has a clear path for your life, and it's time for you to move down a clear road. People change for two reasons either their minds have been opened by God, or because others have broken their hearts, but don't fear change. (Ecclesiastes 3:1)

What does a Godly leader look like?
Christians are called to be leaders if, for no other reason, we are to people as Christ is to the church.
A spouse, manager, or any of the positions of authority are classified as a leader. All leaders in any capacity are expected to reflect godliness the leadership position.
Therefore, I exalt first of all that supplication, prayers, intercession, and giving of thanks be made for all men, for kings and all who are in authority, that we may lead a quiet

and peaceable life in all godliness and reverence. But this is good and acceptable in the sight of God our Savior. The goal of spiritual leadership is that people come to know God and to glorify God in all that he does. Spiritual leadership is aimed not so much at directing people as it is at changing people. If we would be the kind of leaders we are called to be, we must make it our aim to develop persons rather than dictate plans. You can get people to do what you want, but if they don't change in their heart, you have not led them spiritually. You have not taken them to where God wants them to be.

Everyone has the responsibility of leadership in some relationships. But my concern is with the characteristics that a person must have to be a spiritual leader who excels both in the quality of his direction and the numbers of people who follow him. I have always stated that if you look behind you and there's no one following you, you are not leading anybody you are just out for a walk! And you are not leading in your purpose for the church.

The church must do better!

Rev. David Latimore
The Church Must Do Better

THE PURPOSE OF THE CHURCH

Everyone has a purpose. Everything we do that is worthwhile has a purpose. God gave us the church with a purpose in mind. Why is it that so many times the church seems so out of touch?

I think when the world, that's not part of the church, takes a look at us, they see us as second rate, no purpose, no direction. When the world looks at us, it seems like we were developed for bake sales, fish fries, and bingo. Some churches are happier feeding people's stomach and not their souls, but is that what Jesus had in mind when he told Peter, Matthew 16:18-19| "And I tell you that you are Peter, and on this rock, I will build my church, and the gates of Hades will not overcome it. I will give you the keys of the kingdom of heaven; whatever you bind on earth will be bound in heaven, and whatever you loose on earth will be loosed in heaven."

What we need to do is rediscover the truth of what God has already established and then begin to work in that direction. We need to decide what is our driving force. What is it that catches our attention, and what it is that gets us excited. The church must do better!

Rev. David Latimore
The Church Must Do Better

Rev. David Latimore
The Church Must Do Better

Greed

The definition of greed is an inordinate or insatiable longing for material gain, be it food, money, status or power. Today in our society, how important is it to you to have money or a specific type of status, and power? Our society is full of people who strive for the money, the power, and the status no matter what he or she has to do to get it. You hear of people selling their souls for it. Do you not believe that if God wanted you to have those things that he would provide it for you?

There are some who believe that leaders are all about money, nice cars, beautiful homes and the finest of clothing. Don't get me wrong; there's nothing wrong with having those things; it's all about how you acquire them. If you work hard, then you deserve nice things, but if you rely on others to hand you their hard earned money and you're nothing more than a manipulator, then that's where I have to draw the line.

Many people today believe that the majority of churches operate like a business instead of a church. How many years have you heard of your church asking for money for the building fund? It's to the point that the comedians are using this as one of their jokes. How often does your church take up a collection at their Sunday services?

Here's a real example of greed within the church.

There's this no-name church who has a shed, that's what I am going to call it, but it is a part of the church, and the

Rev. David Latimore
The Church Must Do Better

roof is leaking. A young man asked the pastor about the insurance covering the cost of repairs, and he told the young man that the insurance company wouldn't cover it. The young man thought this was strange, so he called a friend of his, that is an insurance agent and explained the situation to the agent. Now, keep in mind that once you file a claim on something it stays in the system forever. The agent told the young man that the church had already filed a claim on this a year ago and was issued a large sum of money to cover the damages, but the church has asked its members for money every Sunday to cover the repairs. Now, how can you call yourself a man or woman of God and lie to your congregation?

Ecclesiastes 5:10| Whoever loves money never has enough; whoever loves wealth is never satisfied with their income.

Hebrews 13:5| Keep your lives free from the love of money and be content with what you have, because God said, "Never will I leave you; never will I forsake you.

Whatever you tell your congregation you're collecting money for, you better use it for that purpose and that purpose only. If you use the money for any other purpose without notifying the congregation why you had to divert the money to another area of the church, and if the members of the church find out they will be highly upset, and they have every right to know. I know someone is saying what you give to the church; the church deserves to use the money any way they see fit. Put this in perspective, if you gave money to a charity foundation and was told they were going to use it to build schools. Then later you found out that they did not use the funds to build schools, but instead, they used the money to buy cars, more than likely you will be less likely to gear at the same rate as you did before because their integrity is at questioned. Remember, 80% of the people who go to your church are not tithers. 20 % takes care of the church, so when the church doesn't do what they say they are going to do, people feel deceived, and that will lead to deception.

Rev. David Latimore
The Church Must Do Better

Rev. David Latimore
The Church Must Do Better

Deception and Fraud

Deception: the act of causing someone to accept as real or invalid an act of deceiving. God is not taking this deception lightly, even if we are. One of the primary deceptions is in finances. Our offering's become a holy thing when we pray over it before we release it to the collection plate/tray in what is known as the church, especially with the pureness of heart and aligned with the spirit of God as well as obedience. In this season of dispensation of time, we have leaders who are deceiving the children (sheep) with their greed, selfish ways by saying, things need repair yet, the funds are redirected towards other means without knowledge, and they may not always be church-related; because they have no accountability, they will not be questioned. Continually lying and attempting to justify the reasoning of the deceit. They will also keep a close-knit circle of yes people who have no conception of church etiquette, but more of a bully mentality and character, wolves in sheep's clothing. They are not in the vein of the Holy Spirit, nor will they allow the Holy Spirit to reign, for the truth of the matter is, they are stealing from the sheep by laying a charge of their lack of understanding and actual knowledge of the word of God. Just as Eli's sons deceived and stole from the children of Israel based on the seat of authority, they were in, and they felt and believed they had the right to do without question and do what pleased them. God showed up and destroyed the sons and raised a true leader where money and deception were not in his heart. False leaders cannot do what is right in the sight of God, so how much more will they do right unto the children of God? The fake leader will always come with a tear and a smile for they dwell in their emotional mindset and throw tantrums when you do not do their bidding. They attempt to make you feel you are in disobedience to God, that you have no right to question, and that you surely cannot judge them according to the word of God with righteous judgment, that you have no ability to discern the deception. But, there is accountability unto the wicked who have robbed the sheep. The church must do better!

Fraud-deliberate deception to secure unfair or unlawful gain, or to deprive a victim of a legal right.

Church crime continues to grow more than 6 percent a year, how is this possible? Because church people can't or refused to believe that their pastor, could steal from the church. Usually, it's the one that's most trusted that will be the one who steals to pay their habits or pay their debt. Using church money for personal reasons is a crime, even if you replace it later.

When a church commits fraud against its congregation, and the public finds out, it makes it hard for people to trust anyone else. Sometimes, this will be a reason people leave the church. Who wants to give their hard earned money to someone to have them use it for one of their many habits. There are many reasons how people can get away with fraud. I was reading an article about some churches where fraud was a big problem. There were three separate cases where Catholic priests in Connecticut are doing time for drug trafficking, obstruction of justice, and embezzlement.

Rev. David Latimore
The Church Must Do Better

There was another case where a priest pled guilty to stealing 1.3 million from the collections. When things like this happen, people try to keep things private, but how can this happen in the house of God? It's puzzling to me. Does it not matter that God sees you and knows your every move? Well, God already knew what you were going to do before you did it.

A young man commented about why people stray from the church, and he said they were probably broke from giving so much money to the church. How can you take money from people who are out here struggling, working hard, and trying to live right by doing what God says by tithing, and in return, the leader of the church is pocketing the money? I wonder if one of their members came to the church to get help because of his or her lights were cut off, would they get help? Probably not, but let the collection get too low, and that will be a sermon by itself.

I read where treasurer of a church embezzled $850, 000 by distributing funds to himself through a credit line. He had access to four officers' digital signatures. His crime led to 8 years in prison, and he was required to pay the money back. Another case where a 55-year-old female embezzled 3,000 but was sentenced to 8 years in prison. These are just some of the cases that have been reported. How many cases go unreported

Here are some things that should raise a red flag when it comes to money within the church.

Rev. David Latimore
The Church Must Do Better

Red flag #1: One person is responsible for it all. Make more than one or two people responsible for it all.

Red flag #2: Counting money alone. At least two or three unrelated people should collect and count the offerings.

Red flag #3. Inadequate supervision. Always reconcile bank statements and monitor financial accounts monthly. The church must do better!

Rev. David Latimore
The Church Must Do Better

Rev. David Latimore
The Church Must Do Better

Conviction

Conviction a firmly held belief or opinion, but by action, it means we have to face the pain of the truth. When asked a simple question as to why I believe people do not attend church, I thought at first; it was going to be a simple task but, when I searched for one answer, it kept changing. I think all of the reasons that I thought I and others like me were not attending; all led to one reason that can be summed up in one-word, conviction. People do many things not to have to face the music. We are doing so much dancing that we don't even realize there is no music playing. Making sure that there is a smile on our face has become more important than ensuring that there is joy in our heart. After all, one is visible for the world to see. We spend so much time and effort appearing to be happy that we do not spend time working on being happy. I often think that this Sunday will be the one day that I go to church, and upon picturing myself sitting on that pew facing my convictions and truths, I cannot drag myself because it will be the one place I cannot wear a smile. It will be the one place; I cannot show snapshots of my life to the world as a beautiful and a happy family woman. It will be the one place where he sees all my pain. And the conviction of his eyes upon me in his house is often more than one can bear. It is the one place where I have to say, "I messed up. I'm screwed up. I'm beautiful on the outside and ugly on the inside. I am hurting. I'm lost. I'm unhappy."
It's the one place you cannot be fake. Most of us have grown up in the church our entire life, and we know the conviction of those words in the bible. We understand what facing them will do to us. It will unclothe us; it will lay

naked our souls. It will show the blackness behind the white smile, and we will be as Adam and Eve and be "AWARE" of our sins. That awareness will make us weep, and though God's hands will wipe our tears, and wrap his arms around us, we know it's a metaphor. We can't touch it, and we struggle to feel it in our hearts without touch. And that is where faith is supposed to kick in, and so we cling to that which is tangible. That's why the sins become the apples. I have no answers as to how to break this cycle. I only know it to be the merry-go-round of my convictions. And so, round and round I go, and when I want the pain to stop, I know where I must go.
So I do not know how you can make it stop for those who are like me in their reasons, but there you are. That's one person's point of view.

Non Believers

Many have stopped believing in our God our Savior. Why is this? Some people think that God doesn't exist because he allows bad things to happen to people. He let the wicked prosper while the believers and faithful ones suffer. So many questions, but if you think back to the biblical days, God allowed his only son to die on the cross for us. Jesus was tormented, and God allowed this, so who are we to question why God allows certain things to happen to people. If he would let his only beloved son experience the pain of the world, we are no better than Jesus, so we too shall experience that pain. The church must do better!

Rev. David Latimore
The Church Must Do Better

Rev. David Latimore
The Church Must Do Better

Hypocrites

Hypocrite- a hypocrite is a person who pretends to have virtues, morals, or religious beliefs, and principles. Could our churches be filled with hypocrites? Well, many people believe so, from the pastor down to the members. Have you ever been to a church and expected warm welcomes, words of encouragement and the only thing you get are mean looks and stares, if so, welcome to the club. People leave churches because this is the one place where you think you can go and people would be sweet, kind and loving, but that's not how most of our churches are. Much evilness and commotion are going on in the churches today from gossiping to adultery. This type of behavior has been going on in the churches for such a long time.

Have you ever noticed how many Christians walk around with the air and haughty demeanor, and lay it to the charge of being a peculiar person, untypical, different, strange, and odd? Most of the time these are your hypocrites hiding behind the partial word of God, This is a disguise to cover up dark moral character, religious beliefs, immoral principles, and character defects so others can not see the real person behind the mask. An actor can only play a role for a short period, and if we are genuinely walking and living the way God wants us to, then the spirit of discernment begins to nudge at the heart whispering, "open up your spiritual eye, pay attention I am showing you the truth." Being hypocritical is merely another form of deceit and a way to manipulate, control, and use the sheep with a lot of glitters and babbling with an appearance of grandeur and success that is ineffective within the buildings known as the church. Your good deeds will not be accounted by

Rev. David Latimore
The Church Must Do Better

the father when the heart is deceitful and full of evil, presenting ourselves as something that we know we're not, is one of the most subtle and dangerous of sins. Romans 1:18| For the wrath of God is revealed from heaven against all ungodliness and unrighteousness of men, who hold the truth in unrighteousness. Romans 3: 20-23| Therefore by the deeds of the law there shall be no flesh, justified in his sight: for by the law is the knowledge of sin. These Leaders give an appearance of righteous living. They are adulterous, liars, deceivers, which is why in this season of time we see where sheep are entering buildings with no respect, murdering spirits, mean-spirited, they have seen the leaders even if the leadership has not realized that they have been exposed. These leaders have no godly compassion to help the sheep. The Hypocrite has become deceived by their actions; they know the word of God but refuse to obey the Word. James 1:22 | States the principle, "But prove yourselves doers of the word, and not merely hearers, who delude themselves." The Hypocrite becomes just like the Jews that Paul confronted; they felt secure before God because of their religious heritage as Jews. They had God's Law; they could confidently teach it to others. But they were deluded because they were hearers of the law, but not doers of it. It is a heart matter, according to Matthew 15:8| People draweth nigh unto me with their mouth and honor me with their lips, but their heart is far from me. But woe unto those who cause the sheep to scatter, hence we now have a generation of unbeliever's, Atheist, Scientology, Stargazers, and youth being shot in the streets, The hypocrite does not care for the well-being of others, not even those that are truly connected to them, due to a waxed cold and harden heart. Again, it is a heart matter, for out of the heart the mouth speaks, and the hand's labor to do evil and not good, they are far too busy covering up the secrets of shame and disgrace they have brought to the body of Christ. They have with their actions lead sheep to the slaughter daily, and daily they continue to do so. Sheep can easily be led astray, and the hypocrite preys on this fact. They know they have not taught the fullness of the word of God, and the sheep have not sought out knowledge, understanding, nor have they asked the Holy Spirit which is our comforter, guide, and director. They are given a false interpretation, expounding, clarification, definition of the real, infallible word of God, so they take it and run, but they are being sent to the slaughter. There is an account as with all things, not unto man, but surely unto God. We as real, infallible leadership must stand rooted firmly in the word and with diligence return the sheep back to the heart of God. We are the burden bearers in this season of time as God continues to unveil the evil altars and hiding places of the hypocrites be its leaders or sheep. We must remember it starts at the head and trickles downward like water.

Rev. David Latimore
The Church Must Do Better

Rev. David Latimore
The Church Must Do Better

The People Voice in the church

I am sure some of you are upset already; however, we don't listen to the people they believe what they see from us. Do you take the time out to listen to the people? Do their opinions, even matter? Over the last several months, I wanted to know what people had to say. So I sent out hundreds of emails to different members of the church community of pastors, deacons, choir members, people who no longer go to church and people who sit in our churches every Sunday, and this is just a few of the comments I received.

Although speaking up can seem scary and even problematic or arrogant, in certain situations it is so crucial that you speak your mind. It will give you self-confidence, promote awareness, educate, stop bullies, and inspire those around you, always speak up. You have more of an impact than you think. Bill Gates once said, "The most unhappy customers are your greatest source of learning."
Of all groups of people, the church must be open and ready to hear those who have been hurt or abused in any way. We can't fool ourselves saying, "If we ignore this it will go away." We must have open ears and hearts to hear the cries of those who are hurt. Of course, we need to listen with discernment and wisdom. And remember an accusation does not always mean an injustice has happened. It is essential that we create an environment where people know they can come, speak, and be heard. It was imperative that I

Rev. David Latimore
The Church Must Do Better

allow people to have a voice in this book that some won't have at their church. People across the country made the following statements.
As I contemplate why people no longer come to church? They don't know God or the truth of his word for themselves. The church looks so much like the world that it repels people because it's hard to see the distinction between the two. I believe that the church (a few exceptions) has become watered down and superficial, and done out of routine opposed to building a relationship with God through Jesus. We don't particularly reverence God the way we should and used to in the past. We tend to minimize his power and authority in our lives. Some preachers that preach to tingle ears are opposed to teaching the true (sound doctrine) that convicts and transforms lives. 2 Timothy. 4:3| We have parishioners who are not intentional in growing spiritually. Some are there for man/preacher, and some are there as a form of religion. The bible states that if I am lifted up, I'll draw all men unto me. |John 12:32
I believe the church should clean house, and get back to teaching basic fundamental principles of sanctification as well as become better disciplines.
Why should people come to church?
It was Jesus' custom, and as followers of Jesus, and being created in his image it should be ours as well. Also, the Bible is clear we should fellowship with other believers. Hebrew 10:19-25| I believe people will find solace, hope, assurance, guidance, healing, forgiveness, grace, and mercy. Most of all, love! Not from man, but God. When we look beyond the frailties of man and see and know God. By Rev Pam B.

Rev. David Latimore
The Church Must Do Better

As we anticipate the return of the Lord for his people, the Bible warns of a great falling away. Because of the lack of knowledge and understanding, many who suppose they are alright out of fellowship with the body of believers. God continually calls the individual into a deeper, more mature walk of faith. God uses his word, his church, other believers, circumstances, prayer, and a host of other vehicles to bring individuals and communities of believers into a close, intimate relationship. [1] The rogue – stand-alone - believer is nowhere to be found in scripture. Excuses of church hurt, and money hungry preachers, are but a couple of the myriad of reasons people use to stay away. The Hebrew writer instructed the body to come together even more often as the Lord's return draws closer. Hebrew 10:25
Cultural, ethnic, socioeconomic, worship styles notwithstanding, members of the body of Christ cannot undermine their responsibility to be a committed participant in the church.
A lack of understanding of the connectedness of the body, as set forth by the apostle Paul in 1st Corinthians 12, has engendered a dangerous epidemic of people who stay away from attending church. However, with so much foolishness and a lack of spiritual in depth going on in so many churches, it is easy to see why someone would decide not to attend. But, in spite of that, each person has to be committed to finding a community of like-minded believers where they can grow and mature in Christ. The "bride" of Christ is not an individual believer, but instead is the collection of believers called "the church." Pastor Lee C

For some, the church is a place that serves as a gathering point to unite with others to enrich the growth and

Rev. David Latimore
The Church Must Do Better

development of their relationship with God. However, as many churches seem to struggle with upholding the values and standards in which their congregation believes, members have lost interest in attending services. Leaders in the church often use their authority to take advantage of their members financially, politically, and emotionally. With so much corruption and abuse perpetrated by these authorities both in my personal experience and around the world, I find it difficult to receive messages of love and Christian values by attending their services. Despite many attempts, it has proven to be nearly impossible to find a church that genuinely embodies Christ, both within the church and in the community.

As someone who finds strength from building a personal and authentic relationship with God, I would instead take the time to read and interpret the Word for myself than assume an interpretation presented by the church. I have sought alternative ways to foster this relationship through fellowship with others that have a real passion for making the world a better place by sharing the love and demonstrating an unconditional acceptance of others. Many regularly attend church without truly living the word of God. To me, it is more important to focus on upholding Christ-like values through everything I do, not just on one day out of the week.
Sent by Sis Naomi

Do you know a church that specializes in feeding peoples stomach and not their souls?
In the movie Simon, he's upset over the conduct of the church. Simon expresses himself in front of everyone.]

Rev. David Latimore
The Church Must Do Better

Simon Birch: I said, "What do coffee and doughnuts have to do with God?"
Rev. Russell: They're merely refreshments so people can socialize and, uh, and discuss the upcoming activities.
Simon Birch: Whoever said the church needs a continental breakfast?
Rev. Russell: -Simon!
Simon Birch: I doubt that God is interested in our church activities.
Rev. Russell: -Simon!
Simon Birch: -If God has made the church bake sale a priority, then I'd say we're all in a lot of trouble.

Does this sound like any church, you know?
From personal experience, many lose hope in the church, but not in God himself. There is still a reference to the supreme deity, but not his proclaimed workers. The church has lost its way as a result of leaders losing their way as well. When one has been taught to reverence the church and its chief earthly officer, it is hard not to know how to see them. Children are taught that their pastor is almost Godlike. This creates a stigma that he is perfect. While as a Christian all must strive to be perfect, but when he falls, it has a greater impact on not only himself but those that follow him.
Another reason many have fallen away from church is there is no real vision for each extension of the body of Christ. How can you follow someone who knows not where he is going? You sell an idea to a group of people, and they then take to the idea. Years down the line when the vision is still in the infancy stage, people begin to lose faith in the vision and ultimately the visionary. By rev Derick J

Rev. David Latimore
The Church Must Do Better

I have heard so many people confidently explain that they saw character issues or problems in the life of the leader months, years, or decades before the sin became public. This prideful declaration betrays our sin of silence. Let's refrain from bragging about what we saw coming. Instead, let's speak up immediately when we see cracks in a leader's character before more lives are damaged. Let's seek to create ministry environments where the gifts of women and men are fully used for the glory of Jesus. God has gifted all people. Wise leaders can have boundaries and still create a place where all gifts are leveraged in all people.

The people's voice:

What would be my reason why I didn't attend church? If I pay a lot of attention to what's going on in the world, it will cause me to be very discouraging. I'm going to believe that there is not a God, so what's the point in going to church because I will ask myself why does God allow all these things to happen. How can he let all the killings go on in the world all over the globe, tornadoes, hurricanes, fires, sickness, and disease? How can God allow all that to go on? Is there a God? Where is God because if it were a God, he wouldn't put us through all this. Why should I choose to attend Church? The word says come unto me, all ye that labor and are heavy laden, and I will give you rest.

Matthew 11:28| But God commendeth his love toward us, in that, while we were yet sinners, Christ died for us."

Rev. David Latimore
The Church Must Do Better

Romans 5:8| Looking around seeing everything that's going on in the world you should say to yourself, I can't afford not to go to Church. We have to have faith the size of a mustard seed is what the word says. We walk by faith and not by sight. God tells us to seek him first, and everything will be added to us.

Attending church does not mean things will be perfect, it's like a big hospital, everyone in there is sick, seeking something from God and to know that all we have to do is have faith and trust him with our whole heart. Attending church should make you feel better than you did when you came. To be amongst people, that's striving just like you to live a better life, should make you feel better at some point. I would rather attend church today knowing I have someone to call on in time of need or to give God thanks for all he has done for us.

The people's voice:

 used to be a church leader, but the day came when I saw how many pastors were not being truthful or living right, so I wanted out. I think many are seeing the same now, but my view is, if God doesn't bother cleaning up the church himself, then why should others. I spent too many years believing for things to change, giving up all my time for over 25 years. God needs to start doing what he says and start making people reap the lies and fraud. God seems not to mind keeping people like this around. A lot of them are lovers of self, more than God or people.

Rev. David Latimore
The Church Must Do Better

The funny thing about it all was, I stopped being broke after I left the church.

It's easy to judge these people for their comments; however, we shouldn't, if this is what they believe, this is what their voice says, so let's look at this and not judge.

Rev. David Latimore
The Church Must Do Better

Rev. David Latimore
The Church Must Do Better

Being Judgmental

Judgmental- Involving the use or exercise of judgment.

For me, church people are the most critical of others new to the body of Christ. I think a lot of times, the church people forget where they were before they were saved. Instead of being a living testimony about where they were and how they overcame, they turn their nose up and act as if they've always been good as gold. If the church is a place of healing, Christians should show more love to those entering. If you're treated better in the streets than you are in the church, why would anyone want to be apart of it?

Men and women of God should think about how he or she treats people. I have heard of stories of people going to a new church, and how some of the members look down on them because they didn't dress as well as some of the members. Some people will never return to a church where the members judge. Is this how God would want us to treat people coming to hear the word of God? Doesn't the bible say come as you are?

Matthew 7:1-5| Do not judge, or you too will be judged. For in the same way you judge others, you will be judged, and with the measure you use, it. Why do you see the speck that is in your brother's eye, but does not notice the log that is in your eye? Or how can you say to your brother, let me take the speck out of your eye, when there is the log in your own eye? You hypocrite, first take the log out of your eye, and then you will see clearly to take the speck out of your brother's eye.

Rev. David Latimore
The Church Must Do Better

Many people in the church who want to talk about what other people are doing, but fail to realize that they are not living a perfect life either. We are not perfect, and we will never be. We will always have some sin in our lives, but don't talk about others when you are the biggest devil in church or at home. On Sunday you're in church praising God, and on Monday through Saturday, you're raising hell and cursing folks out or even worse sleeping with someone's husband or wife. Not many want to serve in a dying church like this.

Rev. David Latimore
The Church Must Do Better

Rev. David Latimore
The Church Must Do Better

Are You Serving in a Dying Church

According to Ed Stetzer, in the entitled come back churches somewhere between 3,500 and 4,000 churches close their doors for the final time every year. Churches, like businesses, ideas, and people, have a life-cycle. They have a time of growth, which is followed by a plateau, which is followed by a decline. If a church doesn't reinvent itself, then it will slide down to its flat-lined: dead.

Aubrey Malphurs, a Senior Professor of Leadership and Pastoral Ministry at Dallas Theological Seminary, explains the cycle by saying, "In general, a church is born, and over time it grows. Eventually, it reaches a plateau, and if nothing is done to move it off that plateau, it begins to decline. If nothing interrupts the decline, it will die."

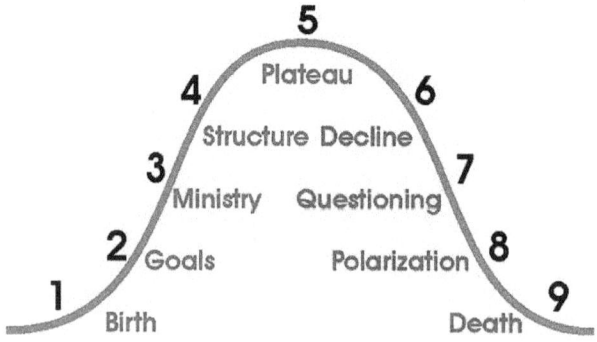

Rev. David Latimore
The Church Must Do Better

At some point on the path of descent, a threshold is crossed that is the point of no return. That point is knocking over the first in a series of dominoes. It starts the beginning of the end, or what Its called "The Domino Effect at a Dying Church."
The first domino is significantly important. What is it? I think the first domino, the one that sets the whole thing in motion, is that the church fails to add even one new member by conversion in a full year.
Drew Goodmanson has found that half of all churches last year did not add one new member through conversion growth. A church's failure to lead people to Christ is just a symptom that indicates a more significant problem: the church is off its mission.

When people who value forward progress (i.e., leaders) begin to recognize that the church is off its mission and has no plans to reinvent itself, they leave to find a place that *is* making forward progress. Even though some churches have been able to reinvent themselves and break out of the decline, leaders sense the particular church doesn't seem poised to do that. Another domino falls.

Because other people follow the leaders, they decide to leave too. The rate of people leaving the church outpaces the percentage of people joining the church, and more dominoes fall.

That exodus of people creates a money shortage that freezes budgets. Quality goes down because you can't keep doing things to the level you were doing them before. Another domino falls.

When quality takes a hit, more people leave. Budgets go from being frozen to being reduced. Quality continues to suffer, only more noticeable now. More people leave, and

Rev. David Latimore
The Church Must Do Better

eventually, a few staff members have to be laid off. I remember a case here in Indianapolis were a church hired a lady named Pat. It wasn't two months later that the church couldn't pay her the salary the leadership team said they were going to pay her, of course, she was told to take a leap of faith and God would provide for her. Not to mention her new salary had dwindled to nothing. The church had no other staff member receiving any pay, not even the pastor, but I deal with the pastors so called none salary later. Some churches had to lay off.

After those staff members are gone, the people who benefited the most from the attention and effort made by those staff members (young families) decided to leave. The people who don't go are usually older people whose kids are out of the house, so they don't mind that the children's ministry has no teacher trained to teach your children effectively and is replaced with an untrained volunteer to lead the kids. The average age of the church rises. What's left is a small congregation with increasing median age. Eventually, they'll pay a pastor and a traditional music minister to provide what is necessary the organizational equivalent to Hospice care until the money finally runs out and all the dominoes have fallen.

This scene is played out at almost 300 churches every month across the United States.

Your Move

If you work at a church that is dying, you have three options:

1) Try to be a change agent.

2) Stay through the slide.

Rev. David Latimore
The Church Must Do Better

3) Leave.

Having been in that position myself, I can tell you that I went with option 1. When that didn't work, I was left with no choice but to go with Option 3. I wasn't willing to try number 2.

Option 3 is safe.

Option 1 is risky.

The option you choose is ultimately up to you.

.

Rev. David Latimore
The Church Must Do Better

Serving in the ministry

Having responsibility without authority

This is a frustrating place to be. Please, if you give someone an area to be responsible for, trust them. Yes, of course, you're still the senior leader, and they need to be accountable, but do not micromanage. If they need permission from you every time a decision is made, you have controlling issues. Let's train our people well enough to be a leader anywhere and not only be a leader at their church. Micromanaging people is never okay under any circumstances, it will rob them of the freedom to grow and decision making. I'm not sure about you, but I would rather have people around me that will decide things instead of always waiting for the decision to be made for them.
This is not only demotivating, but it limits your church growth. Remember your job as a leader is to raise up of the leaders. The church must do better!

Rev. David Latimore
The Church Must Do Better

Rev. David Latimore
The Church Must Do Better

CHANGE IS VERY HARD

Things around us change every day, technology, people, restaurants' changes their menus and we seem to be okay with that. However, anytime we want to change anything in the church it's always drama! Do you remember a company called Blockbuster Video? They were the biggest renter/seller of video and games in the world. Today only one store remains because they were the biggest, they thought no changes were necessary, so a small company called Red Box came in a ran them out of business. Block Buster refused to recognize that change was needed. Don't let your lack of change close your church down!

So if you're holding weekend services, what can you do to bump attendance positively, knowing that it will help people connect better to God?

Here are some ideas that are relatively simple to implement:

1. Invite don't assume

I think many leaders still hold the assumption that if you attend church, you'll be there weekly. As we've seen before, that's not true anymore.

So instead of just closing the service and assuming everyone will be back, invite people to come back. Close the service by saying something like "Next week we'll be (fill in the blank), and we'd love for you to join us."

When you change your language this way, you raise the anticipation level.

2. Facilitate an experience more than a show.

Worship has changed over the last generation, in many ways, it has become as much of a "show" as it has anything else. Millennials are far less attracted to 'the show' (highly produced, highly generic services) than the Boomer baby's parents and grandparents. If you're in a large church, the show will be the experienced killer. People don't want to attend something that they can access just as easily via podcast. If you're a small church, mediocrity (poorly produced, poorly executed services) will be the experienced killer. It's hard to draw people back to something that's consistently underwhelming or poorly done. I think the future will belong to leaders who can facilitate compelling gatherings (large or small) that usher people into the presence of God. Most people want to give themselves to a cause that's bigger than themselves. In my view, no purpose is more significant or more worthy than the mission of the local church.

1. Many churches lose focus on the mission.
2. Volunteering ends up being about filling a slot.
3. Meeting a need and doing your duty.

Or, in the worst case scenario, volunteering can become more about serving the ego of the leader than it does about serving Christ.

When you keep the real mission of the church or your organization central, people rally.

3. Are the relationships around here healthy?

No community should have better relationships than the local church. After all, our faith is based on a Savior who reconciled the world to himself, forgiving our sins. What could we possibly hold against one another? And yet often the local church has some of the most fractious, passive-aggressive relationships out there. We have a Saviour who came full of grace and truth, yet often church leaders will often swing to either extreme: all grace, so issues are never dealt with, or all honesty, so people get hurt. Even if you don't lead a church (leaders from a variety of backgrounds read this blog), realize that many people love the mission of the organization they work for, they can't stand the personal politics and dysfunction.

One of the greatest gifts church leadership can give to a congregation is healthy relationships. So be healthy.

Not sure what that means?

Start by changing one thing. Talk to people you disagree with, not about them. That will change far more than you think. Additionally, almost every organization has toxic people in it. Here's a primer on how to spot and deal with toxic people. Why is the local Walmart better run than the local church? Seriously, one is selling products that last a day, a month, or a year. The other is brokering life change that lasts forever. The church should be the best in the world at recruiting, training and releasing people into ministry and their calling.

4. Work on your welcome

Though this seems incredibly elementary, giving some extra thought to your Sunday Morning Welcome can have a big impact on your community. After leading a church for several years, it can become easy to forget the hesitations of a new church-goer:

1. Will I know anyone?
2. Where should I sit?
3. Have I dressed appropriately?

Making a concerted effort to welcome your new members by name, if possible as soon as they walk through your doors will increase the chance they'll return next Sunday, and the Sunday after that. Seventy nine percent of most churchgoers say this does matter.

Are Your church services lame?

Far too often churches don't grow because the music stinks or the preaching is sub-par, or the nursery is messy, or the programs are disorganized.

We must be willing to speak (and hear) the truth about these things if our churches are going to grow. Our church services must be organized. Our sermons must be compelling. Our buildings must be clean. Our programs must be tight. And don't give me the lame excuse about not having enough budget. For the last 25 years, I have been training teenagers to share their faith through full weekend Dare 2 Share conferences. We've not always had the budget to do everything we've wanted to so that we could produce high-quality events. But, what we've lacked in budget, we've made up for in prayer, creativity, and hard work.

It doesn't take a big budget to have inviting services and tight programs, but it does take a big effort. You and your team must be willing to make that effort!

5. Atmosphere

Every church has an atmosphere, but not all have an atmosphere of friendliness and acceptance. Let's put it bluntly: every church *thinks* it's friendly. But what that often means is they are friendly to each other, and to people they know, friendly to people they like or friendly to people who are like them. I have visited many churches in my days; however, it seems that Mikes car wash has friendlier greeters at the door

6. Unity

Jesus made it clear that unity would be THE verifying mark on his message. A unified church is a growing church, period.

Wanting to stay small. "We like our church just the way it is now." While this attitude usually goes unspoken, it might not even be recognized by its carriers. This is widespread in many churches. The proof of it is seen in how the leaders and congregation reject new ideas and freeze out new people.

There's a lack of accountability for life change. When coaches don't win games, they get fired. When business leaders don't produce a profit, they get fired. We routinely find churches, though, that haven't seen any adult salvations or baptisms in years. As long as the right style of worship with the right length of a message occurs at the right time every Sunday, that's the win. It does not matter if no one is giving their lives to Jesus.

In some denominations, pastors are guaranteed jobs even if their ministry produces no fruit. Where there is no accountability for results, there will never be change.

The only way we will be equipped is if we follow all the other E's of church growth. Evangelism, encourage, edify, exalt....then we are equipped.

The Worst thing you can do when the Spirit has entered the Room

Stop Interrupting the Flow of Worship

We've all been there, and the music is fantastic. The congregation's voices are growing, and eyes closed and hands are raised. Fifteen, thirty, sometimes forty-five minutes go by in a flash because people are meeting God through the experience. It all comes to a crescendo with a closing prayer of thanksgiving and some people wiping away tears. The Spirit powerfully ushered into this place. Then abruptly, the Spirit's asked to sit quietly in the corner for ten minutes so we can take care of some housekeeping. Sometimes that housekeeping is a set of announcements that we could just as quickly read in the weekly bulletin, or it's walking the kids to their Sunday school classes. Sometimes it's a church member making a pitch for more participation in a budding ministry. Whatever the reason for the hiatus, it completely torpedoes the moment. People's hearts have been prepared to hear God's Word and a powerful message. What they get instead is the logistics for the church picnic. Sit down, Spirit. We'll call you when we need you again. Flow matters in a worship service, so make it a priority. Plan it. Choreograph it. It's much better to go from singing to the message than to insert non-worship intermissions.

The church must do better!

What can you do to fix the church?

Surrender to the Holy Spirit

There are two reasons we cannot fix the church: first, because it is compromised of sinners, and second because the Holy Spirit is the one who is doing the work. We can't underestimate his power.

Remember that we are not broken. Reminding ourselves that we are already whole because of Christ refreshes us with the truth that we are not continually searching for something to *fix* us or something in which we find our value and validation. But that's not all. It also reminds us that we cannot use the "We're all broken, imperfect people, so it's fine," excuse anymore. Christ has made us **new**, and we have a given responsibility to live victoriously in that truth (Philippians 1:27).

Over the past week, I've read articles, listened to books, and watched sermons and prayed, and it has me thinking about how we can fix the church. So here's my solution: Here are four ways we can, by the power of the Holy Spirit, actually make a difference in our local churches, and therefore, the universal church.

Rev. David Latimore
The Church Must Do Better

1. Surrender to the Holy Spirit.

2. The church is fixed not by social programs or accountability partners, but by the Spirit. The Holy Spirit is the one doing the work, and although he is gracious enough to let us be included, we need to stop trying to fix the church or fix our own lives without allowing the Spirit to have control. It won't work any other way.

3. Pray for the Spiritual condition of the Church.

No prayer No Change!

The challenge is not just for pastors, elders, or deacons. It's for all of us. We need to pray as Paul does here:

For this reason I bow my knees before the Father, from whom every family in heaven and on earth is named, and that according to the riches of his glory he may grant you to be strengthened with power through his Spirit in your inner being. So that Christ may dwell in your hearts through faith that you, being rooted and grounded in love, may have strength to comprehend with all the saints what is the breadth and length and height and depth, and to know the love of Christ that surpasses knowledge, that you may be filled with all the fullness of God. (Ephesians 3:14-19)

We need to pray not for people to be *fixed*, but for people to be *filled*. Filled with the Holy Spirit, filled with love, which is all in all. It's not about fixing. It's about filling.

Hold a proper view of God and sin to have a thriving church. We need to understand how great our God is. We need to stop belittling him and putting him in the terms that we know.

The Church has surrendered her once lofty concept of God and has substituted it for one so low as to be utterly unworthy of thinking and worshipping men. She has done not deliberately, but little by little and without her knowledge; and her very unawareness only makes her situation all the more tragic. With our loss of the sense of majesty has come the further loss of religious awe and consciousness of the divine presence. We have lost our spirit of worship and our ability to withdraw inwardly to meet God in adoring silence. Modern Christianity is only not producing the kind of Christian who can appreciate or experience the life in the Spirit. The words, "Be still, and know that I am God," mean next to nothing to the self-confident, bustling worshipper in this middle period of the twentieth century.

The middle period of the twentieth century. Doesn't church sound drastically similar to the modern church of the twenty-first century? Many churches dim the reality of the gospel. They tell lies like, "You are worthy, you are essential, you are valuable," and so on, often putting God and us in the same place.

What is so great about us that makes us think that we can be valued, which is what valuable means, anyway?

Being valuable and being valued are two different things. God values us, and in Christ, we are valuable. But apart from Christ, we are not valuable; we are sinners destined to an eternity apart from God. God values us, although we are not able to be valued; although we don't deserve it, God loves us with an everlasting love. He loves his own to the end (John 13:1).

So, of course, we want people to understand how much God loves them and how precious they are to him. But we aren't loved or valued because we deserve it, but because we don't. And that's what makes the truth that we are both loved and valued so priceless.

You can't understand the depths of God's love if you don't understand how massive it is undeserved. Tell people they're unworthy because they are. But they are also worth it, according to Jesus (Hebrews 12:2).

The gospel can lift this destroying burden from the mind, give beauty for ashes, and the garment of praise for the spirit of heaviness. But unless the weight of the burden is felt the gospel can mean nothing to the man; and until he sees a vision of God high and lifted, there will be no woe and no burden. Low views of God destroy the gospel for all who hold them.

4. Own Personal Responsibility

If we want to raise the numbers of millennials in the church since 59 percent of millennials raised in a church drop out, we cannot put all the blame on "the church." We are the church. It is also important to remember that as Christians we ARE the Church. Therefore, we are the imperfection that is, the difference that needs to be, and the good that the Church is doing."

Millennials need to stick around even when they are frustrated or discouraged. We need to build each other up even when we don't get anything out of it. We need to get out of this mentality that we only need to go to church when we feel like it, or the mentality that we do not need "church" at all.

If we didn't need the church, God wouldn't have founded it nor would he have given each person a different gift that is vital for the furthering of the kingdom. In one sermon, Francis Chan challenges us to see the vitality of the church; you can watch this good sermon here.

We need to recognize our responsibility to read the Bible together, pray like Paul discusses in Ephesians 3 and Colossians 1, and have true Christ-honoring fellowship. We need to go back to the Bible and read it for what it is, and not for what we think it should be. The Holy Spirit doesn't just need to be included. He needs to be our one true Guide.

The church will begin to be "fixed" when we start to be filled, but it all starts with our surrendering over to the Holy Spirit. Surrendering happens when we recognize that we can't do it on our own.

The church must do better.

Rev. David Latimore
The Church Must Do Better

Rev. David Latimore
The Church Must Do Better

www.ingramcontent.com/pod-product-compliance
Lightning Source LLC
Chambersburg PA
CBHW051704090426
42736CB00013B/2529